gardening
& planting
by the
mo⦿n
2022

nick kollerstrom

foulsham
LONDON • NEW YORK • TORONTO • SYDNEY

foulsham

An imprint of Foulsham Publishing Ltd

The Old Barrel Store, Drayman's Lane, Marlow, Bucks SL7 2FF

Foulsham books can be found in all good bookshops and direct from www.foulsham.com

Dedicated to the memory of Frau Maria Thun, pioneer of lunar gardening

ISBN: 978-0-572-04817-4

Copyright © 2021 Nick Kollerstrom

Cover photograph © Garden Picture Library

Series, format and layout design © 2021 Foulsham Publishing Ltd

The moral right of the author has been asserted

A CIP record for this book is available from the British Library

Typeset in India by Lapiz Digital Services, Chennai

Printed and bound by CPI Group (UK) Ltd, Croydon, CR0 4YY

Contents

The pull of the Moon is considerable. Not only does it move twice a day, it pulls on the Earth. Many gardeners and farmers are rediscovering the benefit of planting according to its phases, part of a profound knowledge neglected by modern techniques.

Harmony, A New Way of Looking at our World, by HRH The Prince of Wales,
with Tony Juniper and Ian Skelly, 2010, p.137.

Introduction

To everything there is a season and a time to every purpose under heaven; a time to be born and a time to die: a time to plant, and a time to pluck up what is planted...

Ecclesiastes 3: 1–2

here has been, in recent years, a **surge in interest** in home-grown vegetables. While it is delightful to pick food from your own garden, this seems to have combined with a growing suspicion of chemically-treated foods and a desire to say no to genetically-modified commercial produce to inspire more of us to start to grow organic. If you're going to do this, you might as well make use of the rhythms and cycles of Earth, Moon and Sun.

This Calendar, which is based upon many years of practice and research on bio-dynamic farms, has been going for nearly forty years. People like using it and keep using it for one reason: it does really work!

If you would like to explore the subject for yourself, my companion volume *Farmer's Moon* reviews all the evidence from years of work done in fields comparing crop yields from different sowing times. I spent about ten years on these trials in my youth and the results I saw led me to co-author this Calendar. We hear much about the cycle of the Sun these days, mainly because 2019 was quite a deep solar minimum. A new sunspot cycle was meant to begin then but it didn't, which may mean we are coming into a period of a quiet Sun. Some say that will be associated with a time of global cooling. Nobody quite knows at the moment.

Mother Earth has her own rhythms of life, and there is a surprising connection between the Moon and vegetables and the traditional four elements linked to the Moon's journey through the zodiac. Our Calendar uses the traditional zodiac as it has existed in unchanging splendour for 2,500 years, consisting of twelve equal thirty-degree divisions of the sky. We acknowledge the profound effect of the lunar phases upon growth and fertility and, in accordance with tradition, we use the positions of the two most important planets, Saturn and Venus, as well as the rising and setting of the Moon each day, as research has shown that organisms respond to Moonrise.

In today's world, many people do not even know the length of a lunar month. Straightforward information about the lunar effect on the female menstrual cycle remains taboo. I believe all living things respond to the lunar month in their fertility and growth. Ah, if only more people were open-minded enough to attune with the changing Moon, we would enjoy a more gentle and peaceful world.

There is nothing better for reducing stress than contemplating the starry majesty of the night sky and how the Moon moves through it. Try to get to where the night is dark enough and search for the zodiac constellations. Because they're what we are using in this Calendar!

The Four Elements

Clear the sheds of dung, but not at new moon or half moon.

Cato, *On Farming*

 lthough modern lunar gardening guides tend to disagree on many issues, they do concur on one point: they all use a notion of dividing the zodiac into four periods, each connected with a particular element – Earth, Air, Fire and Water. At the core of this calendar is a four-element pattern, generated by the motion of the Moon against the stars, a modern system, based on an ancient idea.

Each month, the Moon moves around the sky against the 12 constellations of the zodiac, each of which has its particular affinity with one of the four elements. Each of the elements has three constellations linked to it, spaced equally around the circle of the zodiac. The diagram below shows the sky-triangles, or trigons, that map the three related signs. The 27-day orbit of the Moon against the stars means that each element lasts for two or three days and is repeated every nine days. The elements of Earth, Water, Air and Fire are said to influence the growth and performance of a particular sort of plant, respectively Root, Leaf, Flower and Fruit-seed. Further division into the well-known 12 signs of the zodiac is secondary in this scheme.

The four-element cycle underlying the zodiac

The theory is that in nature there are four kinds of subtle energy, 'formative forces', which work to influence the way a plant will develop, linking the time of sowing to the final condition of the crop when harvested. These forces are activated by the Moon's passage through the zodiac-elements, as the seed is sown.

The Star Rhythm

The sequence of element days, the star rhythm, runs: Root days, Flower days, Leaf days and then Fruit-seed days.

Root days are the times to sow carrots, potatoes, radishes and other root crops. These days occur when the Moon passes in front of the stars of one of three planets linked to the Earth element: Taurus, Virgo and Capricorn. When this happens, the Moon is said to have an Earth-type energy. If the weather is unsuitable for sowing those particular crops, simply wait for the next set of Root days nine days later.

Root days relate to the Earth signs   *Taurus*   *Virgo*   *Capricorn*

Leaf days are times when the Moon is in front of the constellations related to Water – Cancer, Scorpio and Pisces – and is the time to sow lettuce, cabbage and other leafy crops.

Leaf days relate to the Water signs   *Cancer*   *Scorpio*   *Pisces*

Flower days relate to the Air signs – Gemini, Libra and Aquarius – and are the best times to sow broccoli, globe artichoke, cauliflowers and similar plants.

Flower days relate to the Air signs   *Gemini*   *Libra*   *Aquarius*

Fruit-seed days relate to the Fire signs – Aries, Leo and Sagittarius – and are ideal for sowing tomatoes, beans and peas.

Fruit-seed days relate to the Fire signs   *Aries*   *Leo*   *Sagittarius*

Belief in the Moon's influence on the fertility of plants was once firmly embedded in the consciousness of ancient people and, as this is rediscovered scientifically today, farmers are again coming to regard the application of lunar cycles as a valuable practice.

Gardening Aspects

To the better furthering of the gardener's travails, he ought afore to consider, that the Garden earth be apt and good, wel turned in with dung, at a due time of the year, in the increase of the Moon, she occupying an apt place in the Zodiack, in agreeable aspect of Saturn, and well-placed in the sight of heaven ... for otherwise his care and pains bestowed about the seeds and plants, nothing availeth the Garden.

Thomas Hill, *The Gardener's Labyrinth*, 1577

t Full Moon, we say that the Sun and Moon are in opposition and that means they are on opposite sides of the sky. That is the one day in the month when one rises as the other sets and farmers should enjoy this experience. Two weeks later at New Moon they meet together and the Moon is then invisible, it fades away a couple of days earlier. That meeting is the aspect called conjunction. An aspect is such an angle which expresses a symmetry within the zodiac. In order of decreasing strength, the aspects we here use are:

☌ conjunction (0°)   ◕ solar eclipse (0°)

☍ opposition (180°)   ☽ lunar eclipse (180°)

△ trine (120°)

□ square (90°)

⚹ sextile (60°)

The square and opposition are considered inhibiting and stressful, whereas the trine and the sextile are more beneficial and harmonious.

Each month, the Moon forms these angles or aspects with Saturn and with the other planets. The Moon–Saturn relationship traditionally had particular importance to agriculture and the life of plants. Our calendar indicates most of the Moon–Saturn aspects as they occur, some Moon–Sun aspects when they are relevant, and the aspects between Moon and Venus as they fall on Flower days. The Venus aspects are recommended for working with flowers – sowing, planting out and grafting. In his ever-popular Herbal, Nicholas Culpeper gave this advice about when to pick herbs in terms of finding the right celestial aspects:

'Let them be full ripe when they are gathered, and forget not the celestial harmony before mentioned; for I have found from experience that their virtues are twice as great at such times as others.'

7

Aspects to Saturn

The planet Saturn was traditionally viewed as important for farmers. The Roman god Saturn presided over agriculture (his name is thought to derive from the Latin sator, sower), and the Saturnalia, held just before the winter solstice, was a weeklong, lively agricultural festival in memory of the Golden Age. Indeed classical writers have mentioned no other planet in this regard. In his agricultural poem *Georgics*, Virgil advised, *'Watch the transit of the cold star Saturn'*. Saturn's sickle had a more rustic meaning before it came to denote the limitations of time. In astrological terms, Saturn represents life's challenging, defining and shaping principle. It is also sometimes depicted as Chronos, Old Father Time.

As an example of this traditional view, the sixteenth-century work on gardening lore, *The Gardener's Labyrinth*, explained about sextile aspects between Saturn and the Moon: *'it is then commended to labour the earth, sow, and plant'* whereas, during the square aspect between these two, it was *'denied utterly to deal in such matters'*. The trine was also approved, but the opposition was not.

Much the same advice featured in seventeenth-century British works, for example, *The Whole Art of Husbandry*, while *Dariotus Redivivus* advised that farmers:

'ought to have a special respect to the state and condition of Saturn, that he be not ... afflicted, because he hath chief dominion over husbandry and the commodities of the Earth; let him therefore (if you can so fit it) be in good aspect ... to the Moon.'

For planting crops, the general advice was: *'Plant what you intend, the Moon being either in conjunction, sextile or trine of Saturn.'*

Modern bio-dynamic farmers also consider the lunar opposition to Saturn to be important, so for some time it was the only celestial aspect to feature in their calendar. It is interesting to note that the Foundation for the Study of Cycles, based in Pittsburgh, USA, has found a 29.8-year cycle in famines, a frequency which corresponds almost exactly with the average time it takes Saturn to make one complete revolution through the zodiac.

Our calendar gives the lunar aspects of conjunction, opposition, trine and sextile to Saturn for Leaf, Flower and Fruit-seed days, but not for Root days, as there would be little point in sowing trees and perennial crops on Root days. The harmonious times – trine and sextile – are suitable for sowing perennials and trees, through Saturn's association with long-term cycles, and for increasing the hardiness of plants. Stressful times – conjunction, opposition and square – should be avoided. However, readers may wish to test the belief of bio-dynamic farmers that the opposition is the best Saturn aspect to use.

All aspects are given to the nearest ten minutes GMT (or BST in summer). The best time to sow or plant is between one hour before and half an hour after the aspect occurs, although if that is impossible for practical reasons, sow within six hours before, rather than after, the event.

The Malignity of a Solar Eclipse

The great astronomer Johannes Kepler composed calendars that prognosticated for the year ahead and in one of them (1602) he explained how it all worked. He described an early version of the Gaia theory, whereby the Earth had a vegetable-animal force which had a sense of geometry, which enabled it to respond to the celestial aspects in terms of climate, harvests, good wine years and political stability. Kepler gave an analogy to explain how this worked: just as a peasant could take delight in the piping of a flute without knowing anything about the theory of musical harmony, so the Earth could respond in an unconscious way to the changing geometry of the heavens. The Earth more or less shuddered during an eclipse, he wrote:

'Eclipses ... are so important as omens because the sudden animal faculty of the Earth is violently disturbed by the sudden intermission of light, experiencing something like emotion and persisting in it for some time.'

Early tablets from ancient Babylon testified to the belief in the infertility of the land around the time of an eclipse. As a belief, it has endured longer than most. The early bio-dynamic sowing calendars by Franz Rulni advocated not sowing anything important for several days after an eclipse, while its successor, the modern Thun calendar, gives just the day of an eclipse as not good for planting.

In the Netherlands, there is a garden with a few ragged pear trees which only started to bear small, bitter fruit nine years after they were planted. As a test, they were deliberately planted at the inauspicious moment of a solar eclipse by Karen Hamaker-Zontag, the eminent Dutch astrologer. Let's see more tests done on this phenomenon! That eclipses do diminish seed quality was demonstrated a few decades ago in a series of seed-germination experiments by Theodor Schwenck.

Bio-dynamic Farming

Bio-dynamic farming began back in the 1930s as the very first organic growing movement and it was *holistic*, in other words it focused on how a farm would function as a whole. Today these are the only farms where you will see cows with their horns left on – which is so important for the dignity of the cow, I always feel. Bio-dynamic wines often win top prizes these days.

In my youth I worked on such farms, and I'd frequently hear comments along the lines of 'you can't plant the potatoes today, the Moon isn't right!'. These farms began from lectures given by an Austrian visionary, Rudolf Steiner. What here concerns us is that it was Steiner who explained how there were four basic formative forces that worked in Nature, which were related to the four traditional elements. These were, he said, cosmic-etheric forces, somehow related to the Moon. About twenty years after that, the bio-dynamic farms began to produce Moon calendars.

How to Use the Lunar Calendar

When you cut down elm, pine, walnut and all other timber, cut it when the Moon is waning, in the afternoon, and not under a south wind.

Cato, *On Farming*

his calendar is designed as a practical tool for the gardener and farmer, containing the key information needed on the two monthly cycles for which there is substantial evidence of their effects on gardening: the waxing and waning Moon, and the sidereal 27-day cycle. It also includes other, less well documented but potentially important information about aspects.

Readers may wish to do their own research, sowing some of their crop at an optimal time and more at a negative time to see whether there is any difference in the results. Ideally, a proper experiment requires at least a dozen rows, with equal amounts of seed sown per row on different days, and all harvested in rotation after the same length of time. Over time, one can distinguish lunar patterns from effects created by weather or other influences.

It is not always easy to co-ordinate a gardening schedule to the Moon – we all seem to be so busy these days – but with a little planning it can be achieved, hopefully with a positive effect. Of course, there will always have to be an element of judgement and compromise. For maximum yield, one aims to sow seeds at the peak times of the relevant sidereal energy cycle, yet there is no point in doing so if the ground is too wet, too dry or too cold. Use the following information as a starting point to help you tap into the cosmic influences and improve your crops.

Identifying Your Crops

All plants can be divided into one of four groups, each related to one of the four elements: Earth, Water, Air and Fire.

EARTH
ROOT PLANTS

Asparagus	Horseradish	Onion	Spring onion
Beetroot (red beet)	Jerusalem artichoke	Parsnip	(scallion)
Carrot	Leek	Potato	Swede
Garlic	Mushroom	Radish	Turnip

WATER
LEAF PLANTS

Asparagus	Celery	Fennel	Rhubarb
Basil	Chicory (Belgian	Lettuce	Sage
Bay	endive)	Mint	Sorrel
Brussels sprout	Coriander	Mustard and cress	Spinach
Cabbage	Cress	Parsley	Thyme

AIR
FLOWERING PLANTS

Artichoke	Broccoli	Elderflower
Borage	Cauliflower	Flowering plants

FIRE
FRUIT-SEED PLANTS

Apple	Broad bean	French bean	Plum
Apricot	Cherry	Gooseberry	Pumpkin
Asparagus pea	Courgette	Marrow	Runner bean
Aubergine	(zucchini)	Nectarine	Sweetcorn (corn)
(eggplant)	Cucumber	Pea	Tomato
Blackberry	Fig	Pear	Vine

When to Sow, Cultivate and Harvest

For sowing crops, observe the four-element cycle. In the calendar, these are shown as Root, Leaf, Flower and Fruit-seed days. Use the lists above to identify the day on which your crop should be sown.

If convenient, sowings are best made on the day nearest to the middle of any of the three Moon signs of the appropriate element. Prepare the soil on the same day. Avoid sowing just before the Moon moves out of a sign. Such transition times are given to the nearest hour. In Australia, one of the fathers of bio-dynamics, Alex Podolinsky, advocates sowing just as the Moon enters a new Moon-sign element, so the seed has a full two days in that quality before it changes, on the grounds that it takes that long to germinate. That view may be important in drought-prone countries.

Bio-dynamic farmers believe that any disturbance of the soil should be carried out in the same Moon-sign element in which the seed was sown. Lettuce, for example, is sown on a Leaf day, so its soil preparation as well as subsequent thinning out, weeding and so on should also be done on a Leaf day to enhance the effect.

Both experiments and experience seem to suggest that harvesting as well as sowing should be done on the relevant element days, when the weather permits. For root crops to be stored over winter, harvest on a Root day nearest to the New Moon. Fortunately, there is no hurry in harvesting root crops, so you can usually select an optimum time.

Using the Star Rhythm

If, for practical reasons, you cannot sow at the optimum times, at least try to avoid the worst times. The following diagram shows the regular wave pattern followed by the cycle of the four elements.

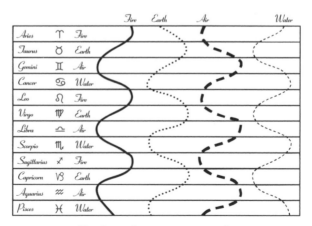

The four-element energy cycles

Root crops, for example, should ideally be sown during Earth days for optimal yield, but if this is impossible, try to avoid planting on days at the trough in the cycle when the Moon is in the opposite element, in this case Water days. The same principle applies to other elements.

The Best Times to Plant
— Moonrise and Moonset

Gardeners are familiar with the idea that the time of day at which certain operations are performed is important. As the celestial element defines the best day for planting, Moonrise or Moonset suggests the best time of day to do the work. The calendar therefore indicates the time of Moonrise and Moonset each day, an hour either side being recommended as the best time to undertake any planting, working or gardening linked to the particular element of the day. Moonrise occurs in the daytime during the waxing phase, so this time is given for these dates. In the waning phase, Moonset occurs during the day, so this time is given. Thus Moonrise just before Full Moon happens in late afternoon. On the day of Full Moon, the Moon rises as the Sun sets.

Moonrise times are given for zero degrees longitude. For any other longitude, obtain the time of rising by adding one hour per 15 degrees of longitude due west. If your position is three degrees due west, for example, add 12 minutes to the times given in the calendar. Also the Moon rises earlier due north. Readers in other latitudes can check this by watching the Moon rise and comparing the time of day to that given here.

Moonrise and Moonset are especially significant if a relevant aspect is being formed by the Moon that day, for example with the Sun or Saturn.

Laboratory research by US biologist Frank Brown has demonstrated that the greatest metabolic rate in both plants and small animals was registered at the times of Moonrise and culmination, when it reaches its highest point in the sky about six hours later. US traditions take these as the best times of day for fishing.

For effective lunar planting, seed should really begin to germinate as soon as it is sown by beginning to absorb moisture from the soil; so it is preferable, at least in warm weather, to sow seeds in the afternoon when the soil will remain moist for longer after sowing.

Planting out crops is, in general, best done in the evening so they have the night to settle in and rest, while pruning is best done in the morning so that the Sun will dry up the cut surface, thereby inhibiting bleeding. Traditionally, crops were harvested in the morning.

Grafting is generally a spring activity and pruning is one for late autumn and winter.

It is also recommended that pruning should be done on the waning Moon and grafting on the waxing Moon. Planting out should be done in the waxing Moon, if possible in the same element in which the sowings were made.

The Harmony of a Sun–Moon Trine

The calendar gives the trine (120º) angle between Sun and Moon, as happens twice a month. This is a harmonious aspect free of stress or conflict. Its moment of linking the two luminaries is a good time for many things. Like the event of Moonrise, it seems never before to have featured in a UK lunar-gardening guide: the idea came from the American book *Gardening Success with Lunar Aspects* by Adèle Barger (1976). This aspect is of particular interest for crops ruled by the Sun, for example oranges or vines.

Growing Flowers

For Flower days, the aspects between the Moon and Venus are given. A Moon–Venus energy is ideal for sowing or planting flowers, especially roses, which are ruled by Venus. The square aspects are also included, even though some might view them as unsuitable, expressing difficulty and stress. Alternatively, they could be viewed as assisting the development of structure, so it is up to you to choose.

Trees and Perennials

When working with trees or woody plants, choose a Saturn aspect for the most propitious time. The calendar gives three types of Moon–Saturn aspect each month: the opposition (180º), the trine (120º) and the sextile (60º). Growers should be mainly concerned with the Saturn aspects on Fruit-seed days, as most of their trees will be fruit-bearing. Because trees are going to last for years, there is all the more reason to identify the optimal date for planting. There may be a choice here: if planting a honeysuckle or clematis to grow up a wall, choose a Flower day, then look for either a Saturn aspect for durability or a Venus aspect for pretty flowers.

How to Read the Calendar

Each page is devoted to a single week, and each day provides all the essential information to help you make the most of your lunar gardening, indicated by various symbols. Each piece of information will be found in the same position on the daily calendars so they will soon become familiar. The calendar gives practical notes for the days to help your understanding of the aspects given, and makes suggestions on gardening activities. The notes also give the sacred Moons, such as when Easter falls or the Jewish New Year begins. Notice that the Muslim months begin a day or two after the actual New Moon, and these beginning days should be when you can first see the thin crescent of the New Moon at dusk. There's also space to record your own gardening notes.

The following symbols are used on the calendar. The key is repeated throughout the calendar along the bottom of the pages for easy reference.

Elements
These indicate the type of crop to sow on the relevant days.

 Earth – Root days   Air – Flower days

 Water – Leaf days   Fire – Fruit-seed days

Sidereal Signs
These show the zodiac sign relevant to the day, and the time at which the Moon moves into the next sign.

♈	Aries (Fire)	♎	Libra (Air)
♉	Taurus (Earth)	♏	Scorpio (Water)
♊	Gemini (Air)	♐	Sagittarius (Fire)
♋	Cancer (Water)	♑	Capricorn (Earth)
♌	Leo (Fire)	♒	Aquarius (Air)
♍	Virgo (Earth)	♓	Pisces (Water)

Moon Phases
Times are given next to the Moon symbols.

● New Moon   ○ Full Moon

◐ Waxing Moon, first quarter   ◑ Waning Moon, third quarter

Moonrise and Moonset
Although this is not part of an ephemeris, times are given for Moonrise for the waxing Moon and Moonset for the waning Moon, as these occur during the day.

☽ Moonrise   ☾ Moonset

Aspects
Conjunction, opposition and square are considered negative aspects. Trine and sextile are considered positive aspects.

☌	Conjunction (0º)	☀	Solar Eclipse (0º)
☍	Opposition (180º)	☋	Lunar Eclipse (180º)
△	Trine (120º)	□	Square (90º)
✳	Sextile (60º)		

Specific aspects are given that relate to Saturn, Venus and the Sun.

♄ Saturn   ☉ Sun

♀ Venus

Nodes

These are the points at which the Moon crosses the ecliptic.

☊   North node   ☋   South node

Apogee and Perigee

The apogee is the time at which the Moon is furthest from the Earth in its orbit, the perigee is when it is closest to the Earth.

$\mathcal{A}$ Apogee $\mathcal{P}$ Perigee

Understanding the Entries

Here are a couple of examples, showing how to read the daily entries.

Wednesday 24	♑	
Sow swedes or hardy turnips.	○ 09.00	
	☽ 20.40	

This is a Root day because the Moon is in Capricorn, an Earth constellation, shown by the zodiacal glyph on the left. The Moon-quarter symbol indicates that this is a Full Moon, its time to the nearest hour noted next to the symbol. The time of Moonrise, to the nearest ten minutes, is given next to the crescent.

Tuesday 27	♓ 12.00 ♈	
		Change 12.00
	☾ 09.40	
	☾ ✶ ♄ 18.00	

The transition from one zodiac sign to another, the ingress, occurs at noon. As the Moon progresses through the zodiac, so the ruling elements shift according to the same timetable, so the morning is Pisces, a Water sign giving a Leaf day, while the afternoon is Aries, a Fire sign, giving a Fruit-seed day. Moonset is at 09.40, then in the afternoon there is a Moon-Saturn sextile (60°) aspect, which is good for trees.

Checklist for Using the Calendar

Annual crops

Follow the four-element rhythms, sowing as near to the centre of the relevant sign as is convenient. The same element-sign (Root, Leaf, Flower, Fruit-seed) reappears every nine days, so if you miss the appropriate period the next may still be convenient.

Grafting and transplanting
Try to do this kind of activity under a waxing Moon.

Harvesting
Fruits picked at New Moon will store better, whereas fruits to be eaten fresh are best picked at Full Moon. Crops should be harvested in the same Moon-sign element in which they were sown if you wish to obtain seeds for next year's crop.

Perennial crops, shrubs or trees
Try to take advantage of a Saturn–Moon aspect when planting. If a tree or bush is fruit-bearing, you can also try to plant or graft it on a Fruit-seed day.

Pruning and gelding
The lunar water uptake cycle is relevant here and near Full Moon is not recommended for pruning; try to time such activity for the waning Moon.

Sowing times
Sow and plant as close to the hour of Moonrise as possible, with adjustments to your longitude and latitude. Avoid sowing for a few hours either side of the nodes, the perigee or an eclipse. Where drought is a problem, note that seeds tend to absorb the greatest amount of water on the days prior to the Full Moon, so sowing at this time should lead to optimal germination.

Times and Time Zones

All times are given in the 24-hour clock. Aspect times are given to the nearest ten minutes, Moonrise and Moonset times to the nearest ten minutes and other times to the nearest hour.

All times are GMT, or British Summer Time (BST, 1 hour added). Users in other parts of the world will need to adjust the times according to their time zone, adding or subtracting the number of hours given below.

Time Zone Adjustments for North America		Time Zone Adjustments for Australasia	
Atlantic	-4 hours	New Zealand	+12 hours
Eastern	-5 hours	Western Australia	+ 8 hours
Central	-6 hours	Southern Australia	+ 9½ hours
Mountain	-7 hours	Northern Territory	+ 9½ hours
Pacific	-8 hours	New South Wales	+ 10 hours
Yukon	-9 hours	Victoria	+ 10 hours
Alaska-Hawaii	-10 hours	Queensland	+ 10 hours
Bering	-11 hours	Tasmania	+ 10 hours

October 2021

October Reminders

Friday 1
Prune trees in the waning Moon.

♋

☾ ✳ ☉ 18.30

☾ 16.40

Saturday 2
Clear leaves and decaying plants away to the compost heap.

♋ 23.00 ♌

☾ 17.00

Sunday 3
Harvest festival is usually celebrated this first Sunday of October.

♌

☾ 17.30

● New Moon	◗ 1st quarter	☽ Moonrise	♌ North node	∂ Apogee
○ Full Moon	◑ 3rd quarter	☾ Moonset	℧ South node	℘ Perigee

October 2021

Monday 4
Pick fruit crops to store over winter.

♌

☾ 17.50

Tuesday 5
Harvest root crops for storage.

♌ 04.00 ♍

☾ ⚹ ♀ 09.50

☾ 18.10

Wednesday 6

♍

● 12.00

Thursday 7

♍ 06.00 ♎

☽ 08.20

Change 06.00

Friday 8

♎

☽ 09.50

℘ 18.00

AM only

Saturday 9
Prepare new rose beds for planting in the morning.

♎ 07.00 ♏

☊ 21.00

☽ 11.10

AM only

Sunday 10

♏

☽ 12.30

♈	♉	♊	♋	♌	♍
Aries	Taurus	Gemini	Cancer	Leo	Virgo
Fire	*Earth*	*Air*	*Water*	*Fire*	*Earth*

October 2021

Monday 11

♏ 08.00 ♐

☽ 13.40

Change 08.00

Tuesday 12

Graft fruit-trees and cut out fruited blackberry and loganberry canes.

♐

☽ 14.40

Wednesday 13

♐ 12.00 ♑

☾

☽ 15.20

AM

PM

Thursday 14

♑

☽ ☌ ♄ 09.50

☽ 15.50

☽ ⚹ ♀ 11.00

Friday 15

♑ 17.00 ♒

☽ △ ☉ 13.30

☽ 16.20

Change 17.00

Saturday 16

The Sun passes by Spica today, the benevolent star of the grain harvest. It brings abundance and good fortune by tradition.

♒

☽ 16.40

Sunday 17

Continue preparing new rose-beds for planting or plant some lily of the valley.

♒

☽ 17.00

♎	♏	♐	♑	♒	♓
Libra	Scorpio	Sagittarius	Capricorn	Aquarius	Pisces
Air	Water	Fire	Earth	Air	Water

October 2021

Monday 18

Start planting winter lettuce. Force-grow rhubarb in a warm greenhouse. Admire the big, yellow Hunter's Moon coming up.

♒ 00.00 ♓

☽ 17.20

Tuesday 19

Plant herbaceous perennials and deciduous trees, but avoid frosty conditions.

♓

☽△♀ 11.40

☽ 17.30

Wednesday 20

The Hunter's Moon, a name that may be somewhat politically incorrect today! Stroll out in the evening to enjoy it.

♓ 10.00 ♈

○ 16.00

Change 10.00

Thursday 21

♈

☾ 08.20

Friday 22

Pick late tomatoes and let them ripen in trays. Work on any fruit trees at noon.

♈ 21.00 ♉

☾ 09.30

Saturday 23

♉

☊ 13.00

☾ 10.40

No Planting

X

Sunday 24

Dig up maincrop potatoes, lift and store beetroot, and harvest root crops for storage.

♉

☾ 11.40

♃ 16.00

♀ Venus   ☉ Sun   △ Trine   ♂ Conjunction   ☌ Solar eclipse

♄ Saturn   ☐ Square   ✳ Sextile   ☍ Opposition   ☍ Lunar eclipse

October 2021

Monday 25	♂ 10.00 ♊	
	☽ 12.40	Change 10.00
Tuesday 26 Prune rambler roses and plant out bulbs on rock gardens or between herbaceous plants.	♊ ☽ 13.20	
Wednesday 27	♊ 23.00 ♋ ☽ 14.00	
Thursday 28 Prune and tend to trees today. Prune any late vines in early afternoon when the half-Moon sets.	♋ ◐ ☽ 14.40	
Friday 29 Venus is at maximum elongation – it appears furthest from the Sun in the evening sky, a good time to view.	♋ ☽ 15.00	
Saturday 30	♋ 08.00 ♌ ☽ △ ♀ 08.00 ☽ 15.30	Change 08.00
Sunday 31 Today is Halloween, tradiitionally a time of other-worldly interference in human affairs. BST ends and clocks go back one hour.	♌ ☽ ⚹ ☉ 09.00 ☽ 14.50	

● New Moon	◐ 1st quarter	☽ Moonrise	☊ North node	⍺ Apogee
○ Full Moon	◑ 3rd quarter	☾ Moonset	☋ South node	℘ Perigee

November 2021

Monday 1
All Saints' Day

♌ 13.00 ♍

☾ 15.10

AM

PM

Tuesday 2

♍

☾ △ ♄ 11.30

☾ 15.30

Wednesday 3

♍ 15.00 ♎

☾ 15.50

Change 15.00

Thursday 4
The Indian festival of Diwali begins, to celebrate the conquest of good over evil.

♎

● 21.00

☾ 16.20

Friday 5
Bonfire night

♎ 16.00 ♏

☽ 07.40

ℙ 22.00

AM only

Saturday 6
Plant trees and bushes. Soak dry tree roots before planting, and prune fruit trees after planting. Stake trees.

♏

☊ 04.00

☽ 09.10

☽ ✳ ♄ 12.50

PM only

Sunday 7
The pagan quarter-day of Samhain: a gathering of the clans before winter begins.

♏ 16.00 ♐

☽ 10.20

Change 16.00

♈	♉	♊	♋	♌	♍
Aries	Taurus	Gemini	Cancer	Leo	Virgo
Fire	Earth	Air	Water	Fire	Earth

November 2021

Monday 8
♐

Diwali ends. Prune fruit trees in the afternoon. Plant gooseberry bushes and raspberry canes. Sow round-seeded peas.

☽ 11.30

☽ ☌ ♀ 05.20

Tuesday 9
♐ 17.00 ♑

☽ ✳ ☉ 05.10

☽ 12.20

Change 17.00

Wednesday 10
♑

☽ ☌ ♄ 16.10

☽ 13.00

Thursday 11
♑ 21.00 ♒

Check over any stored corns or tubers for signs of mould.

◐

☽ 13.20

Friday 12
♒

Cut back and tidy any flowering plants. In the greenhouse, start forcing bulbs and sow seeds of most alpines around 1–2 pm.

☽ 13.50

Saturday 13
♒

☽ 14.10

Sunday 14
♒ 05.00 ♓

☽ 14.20

Change 05.00

♎	♏	♐	♑	♒	♓
Libra	Scorpio	Sagittarius	Capricorn	Aquarius	Pisces
Air	Water	Fire	Earth	Air	Water

November 2021

Monday 15

Take cuttings of bay and rue and place in pots of sand; divide roots of mint, re-potting some for the greenhouse.

♓

☽ 14.40

☽ ✶ ♄ 07.00

Tuesday 16

♓ 15.00 ♈

☽ 15.00

Change 15.00

Wednesday 17

♈

☽ 15.20

Thursday 18

♈

☽ 15.40

Friday 19

Partial lunar eclipse of the setting Moon near the time of the sunrise. No gardening today.

♈ 03.00 ♉

☊ 18.00

☉ ☾ 09.00

No Planting

X

Saturday 20

Finish digging new beds and borders for winter weathering.

♉

☾ 08.30

☾ △ ♄ 07.10

Sunday 21

♉ 16.00 ♊

☾ 09.30

♃ 02.00

Change 16.00

♀ Venus	☉ Sun	△ Trine	♂ Conjunction
♄ Saturn	☐ Square	✶ Sextile	☍ Opposition

♂ Conjunction ● Solar eclipse
☍ Opposition ● Lunar eclipse

November 2021

Monday 22

Prick out any perennials you have raised in the greenhouse and sow winter bedding plants.

♊

☾ 10.20

Tuesday 23

♊

☾☍♀ 10.50

☾ 11.00

Wednesday 24

Make a compost bin for all the leaves raked up in the garden.

♊ 04.00 ♋

☾ 11.40

Thursday 25

Plant new hedges, shrubs and trees.

♋

☾ 12.10

Friday 26

♋ 15.00 ♌

☾ 12.30

Change 15.00

Saturday 27

♌

◑

☾ 12.50

Sunday 28

Advent Sunday; Christmas decorations can go up now.

♌ 23.00 ♍

☾△♀ 13.10

☾ 13.10

● New Moon   ◐ 1st quarter   ☽ Moonrise   ☊ North node   𝒜 Apogee

○ Full Moon   ◑ 3rd quarter   ☾ Moonset   ☋ South node   𝒫 Perigee

November 2021

Monday 29

Finish digging new beds and
borders for winter weathering.

♍

☾ 13.30

Tuesday 30

St Andrew's Day is celebrated in
Scotland.

♍

☾ 13.50

Gardening Notes

♈	♉	♊	♋	♌	♍
Aries	Taurus	Gemini	Cancer	Leo	Virgo
Fire	*Earth*	*Air*	*Water*	*Fire*	*Earth*

December 2021

December Reminders

Wednesday 1

Continue pricking out perennials in the greenhouse and sowing winter bedding plants.

♍ 02.00 ♎

☾ 14.10

Thursday 2

Work on flowers in the greenhouse, taking cuttings and potting. Set them around 2–3 pm.

♎

☾ 14.40

Friday 3

♎ 03.00 ♏

☊ 15.00

☾ 15.20

No Planting

✕

Saturday 4

Total solar eclipse. Stay out of the garden today.

♏

●◕ 08.00

☽ 08.00

ℙ 10.00

No Planting

✕

Sunday 5

♏ 02.00 ♐

☽ 09.10

♎	♏	♐	♑	♒	♓
Libra	Scorpio	Sagittarius	Capricorn	Aquarius	Pisces
Air	Water	Fire	Earth	Air	Water

December 2021

Monday 6
St Nicholas's Day. Cut down old raspberry canes in the morning.

♐

☽ 10.10

Tuesday 7
Venus is most brilliant in the evening sky.

♐ 02.00 ♑

☽ 10.50

Wednesday 8
Sow carrots in frames.

♑

☽⚹☉ 16.00

☽ 11.30

Thursday 9

♑ 05.00 ♒

☽ 11.50

Change 05.00

Friday 10
Prune back established rose-beds. Plant shrubs if the winter weather permits.

♒

☽ 12.10

Saturday 11

♒ 11.00 ♓

☽⚹♀ 12.50

◑

☽ 12.30

Change 11.00

Sunday 12
Dig soft vegetable waste into trenches.

♓

☽⚹♄ 16.50

☽ 12.50

| ♀ Venus | ☉ Sun | △ Trine | ♂ Conjunction | ◖ Solar eclipse |
| ♄ Saturn | ☐ Square | ⚹ Sextile | ☍ Opposition | ◗ Lunar eclipse |

December 2021

Monday 13

The Geminids meteor shower may reach its maximum during this dark night, weather permitting.

♓ 21.00 ♈

☽ 13.10

☽ △ ☉ 16.00

Tuesday 14

Cut down old raspberry canes.

♈

☽ 13.20

Wednesday 15

Sow melons for an early crop and tomatoes for a summer crop if the weather permits.

♈

☽ 13.50

Thursday 16

♈ 09.00 ♉

☽ 14.10

☽ △ ♀ 13.10

Change 09.00

Friday 17

The Saturn aspect in the evening is a good time to plant deciduous trees.

♉

☽ 14.40

☊ 00.00

PM only

☽ △ ♄ 18.00

Saturday 18

Examine stored vegetables and remove any that are diseased.

♉ 22.00 ♊

☽ 15.20

𝒜 02.00

Sunday 19

Pot autumn-sown sweet peas. Prune back established rose-beds.

♊

○ 05.00

☾ 08.20

● New Moon ◐ 1st quarter ☽ Moonrise ☊ North node 𝒜 Apogee
○ Full Moon ◑ 3rd quarter ☾ Moonset ☋ South node 𝒫 Perigee

December 2021

Monday 20

♊

☾ 09.00

Tuesday 21

Winter Solstice at 3.58 pm, the shortest day and longest night. The Sun crosses over the Galactic Equator in its yearly path.

♊ 10.00 ♋

☾ ☍ ♀ 14.40

☾ 09.40

Change 10.00

Wednesday 22

♋

☾ 10.10

Thursday 23

Trim back lawn edges to make the garden tidy.

♋ 21.00 ♌

☾ 10.40

Friday 24

A lovely Sun–Moon trine just before Christmas!

♌

☾ △ ☉ 14.00

☾ 11.00

Saturday 25

Christmas Day and the twelve Holy Nights begin.

♌

☾ 11.20

Sunday 26

Boxing Day starts off with a harmonious Moon–Venus aspect.

♌ 06.00 ♍

☾ △ ♀ 08.10

☾ 11.40

Change 06.00

♈	♉	♊	♋	♌	♍
Aries	Taurus	Gemini	Cancer	Leo	Virgo
Fire	*Earth*	*Air*	*Water*	*Fire*	*Earth*

December 2021

Monday 27
Substitute Bank Holiday for Christmas Day.

♍

☽ △ ♄ 13.00

◑

☽ 11.50

Tuesday 28
Substitute Bank Holiday for Boxing Day.

♍ 11.00 ♎

☽ □ ♀ 12.20

☽ 12.10

Change 11.00

planted Garlic @ 11am

Wednesday 29

♎

☽ ⚹ ☉ 10.40

☽ 12.40

Thursday 30

♎ 14.00 ♏

☽ ⚹ ♀ 13.20

☽ 13.10

AM

PM

Friday 31
New Year's Eve (Hogmanay in Scotland).

♏

☊ 01.00

☽ 13.50

☽ ⚹ ♄ 18.10

PM only

Gardening Notes

♎	♏	♐	♑	♒	♓
Libra	Scorpio	Sagittarius	Capricorn	Aquarius	Pisces
Air	Water	Fire	Earth	Air	Water

January 2022

January Reminders

Saturday 1
New Year's Day

♏ 14.00 ♐

☾ 14.40

♇ 23.00

AM only

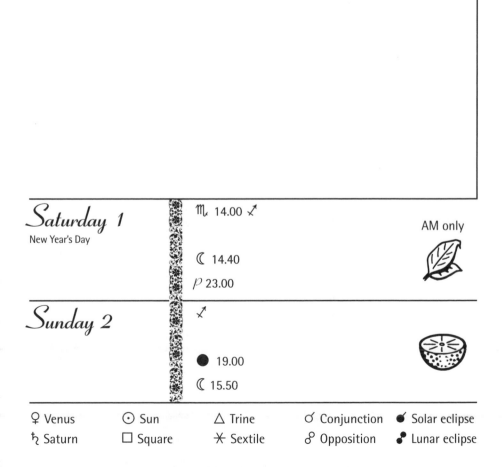

Sunday 2

♐

● 19.00

☾ 15.50

♀ Venus	☉ Sun	△ Trine	♂ Conjunction	● Solar eclipse
♄ Saturn	☐ Square	✳ Sextile	☍ Opposition	☊ Lunar eclipse

January 2022

Monday 3
Venus, the Evening Star, fades from view to meet the Sun in a few days' time. Substitute New Year's Day bank holiday.

♐ 13.00 ♑

☽ 08.40

☽ ☌ ♀ 10.00

AM

PM

Tuesday 4
Perihelion at 7 am, as the Earth reaches its nearest point to the Sun in midwinter. Substitute Bank Holiday in Scotland for 2nd January.

♑

☽ 09.20

☽ ☌ ♄ 18.40

Wednesday 5
Twelfth Night, the last of the Holy Nights of Christmas.

♑ 14.00 ♒

☽ 09.50

AM

PM

Thursday 6
Epiphany, when gifts of Gold, Frankincense and Myrrh were brought by the three Magi (astrologers) to the baby Jesus.

♒

☽ 10.20

Friday 7
A good day to work in the greenhouse, with two harmonious sextile aspects.

♒ 19.00 ♓

☽ 10.40

☽ ⚹ ☉ 05.40

☽ ⚹ ♀ 10.40

Change 19.00

Saturday 8
Venus meets the Sun in our sky today.

♓

☽ 10.50

Sunday 9
Cut out any dead or diseased wood from fruit trees.

♓

◑

☽ 11.10

☽ ⚹ ♄ 05.30

● New Moon   ◐ 1st quarter   ☽ Moonrise   ☊ North node   𝒜 Apogee

○ Full Moon   ◑ 3rd quarter   ☾ Moonset   ☋ South node   𝒫 Perigee

January 2022

Monday 10

♓ 03.00 ♈

☽ 11.30

Tuesday 11

♈

☽ 11.50

Wednesday 12

♈ 15.00 ♉

☽△☉ 11.20

☽ 12.10

Change 15.00

Thursday 13

Spread compost on empty ground.

♉

☊ 04.00

☽ 12.40

PM only

Friday 14

Venus re-appears as the Morning Star on around this date.

♉

☽△♄ 06.30

☽ 13.20

𝒜 09.00

Saturday 15

♉ 04.00 ♊

☽ 14.00

Sunday 16

Plant hardy perennials, using the Moonrise hour of 3 pm.

♊

☽ 15.00

♈	♉	♊	♋	♌	♍
Aries	Taurus	Gemini	Cancer	Leo	Virgo
Fire	*Earth*	*Air*	*Water*	*Fire*	*Earth*

January 2022

Monday 17
Notice how high the Full Moon rises in the midnight sky!

♊ 17.00 ♋ *cleaned up the indoor bed. Wed*
○ 24.00 *worm juice*
☽ 16.00 *outside too*

Change 17.00

Tuesday 18
Erect training wires ready for spring climbers.

♋

☽ 08.10

Wednesday 19
Sow salad crops in the greenhouse or in plastic cloches.

♋

☽ 08.40

Thursday 20

♋ 03.00 ♌

☽ 09.00

Friday 21
Plant a small fruit tree if you have room in your garden.

♌

☽ △ ♀ 13.20

☽ 09.20

Saturday 22

♌ 11.00 ♍

☽ 09.40

garlic planted. 2pm.

Change 11.00

Sunday 23

♍

☽ 10.00

♎	♏	♐	♑	♒	♓
Libra	Scorpio	Sagittarius	Capricorn	Aquarius	Pisces
Air	*Water*	*Fire*	*Earth*	*Air*	*Water*

January 2022

Monday 24

♍ 18.00 ♎

☾ 10.20

Change 18.00

Tuesday 25

Burns Night. *My love is like a red, red rose...* Enjoy some haggis to mark the occasion.

♎

◑

☾ 10.40

Wednesday 26

Keep Christmas bulbs moist but not wet, and in good light for the best flowers.

♎ 22.00 ♏

☾ 11.10

Thursday 27

♏

☊ 06.00

☾ 11.40

PM only

Friday 28

If weather permits, clear dead material from leafy plants.

♏ 24.00 ♐

☾ ⚹ ♄ 08.40

☾ 12.30

Saturday 29

♐

☾ 13.30

Sunday 30

♐

☾ 14.40

♇ 07.00

PM only

♀ Venus	☉ Sun	△ Trine	☌ Conjunction	● Solar eclipse
♄ Saturn	□ Square	⚹ Sextile	☍ Opposition	☋ Lunar eclipse

January 2022

Monday 31

 ↗ 00.00 ♑

☾ 16.00

Sow or tend to any root crops around 4 pm. Work the ground ready for planting.

Gardening Notes

February 2022

Tuesday 1
Chinese New Year of the Tiger.

♑

☽ ♂ ♄ 11.00

● 06.00

☽ 07.50

Wednesday 2
Candlemas, the old English quarter-day. Also Groundhog Day in America for making predictions on the arrival of spring.

♑ 01.00 ♒

☽ 08.10

Thursday 3
The pagan fire-festival of Imbolc marks the first promise of spring. Enjoy a log fire.

♒

☽ ✶ ♀ 06.30

☽ 08.40

Friday 4
Explain to your friends that spring has now begun – even though it may not feel that way!

♒ 05.00 ♊

☽ 09.00

Change 05.00

Saturday 5

♊

☽ 09.20

Sunday 6

♊ 12.00 ♈

☽ 09.30

AM

PM

♈	♉	♊	♋	♌	♍
Aries	Taurus	Gemini	Cancer	Leo	Virgo
Fire	Earth	Air	Water	Fire	Earth

February 2022

Monday 7
Sow early peas and broad beans in a sheltered south-facing area.

♈

☽ 09.50

Tuesday 8
Complete sowing of early peas and beans, under cloches if necessary, around 10–11 am.

♈ 23.00 ♉

◑

☽ 10.20

Wednesday 9

♉

☊ 06.00

PM only

☽ 10.40

Thursday 10

♉

☽ 11.20

Friday 11
Get up early this week to see Venus shining brilliantly in the early morning sky.

♉ 12.00 ♊

☽ △ ☉ 08.20

AM

☽ 12.00

PM

𝒜 03.00

Saturday 12
Bring in bulbs for indoor flowering as they become ready.

♊

☽ 12.50

Sunday 13
Start some early protected cauliflowers today, sowing them around 2 pm.

♊ 24.00 ♋

☽ ☍ ♀ 05.50

☽ 13.50

♎	♏	♐	♑	♒	♓
Libra	Scorpio	Sagittarius	Capricorn	Aquarius	Pisces
Air	Water	Fire	Earth	Air	Water

February 2022

Monday 14
♋

☽ 14.50

Tuesday 15
Buddhist Nirvana Day: wish peace to all sentient beings.

♋

☽ 16.00

Wednesday 16
♋ 10.00 ♌

○ 17.00

Change 10.00

Thursday 17
Tend to fruit trees today.

♌

☾ 07.30

Friday 18
♌ 17.00 ♍

☾ △ ♀ 05.50

☾ 07.50

Change 17.00

Saturday 19
Trim back and begin to water fuchsia and pelargonium roots to encourage them back to life.

♍

☾ 08.10

Sunday 20
♍ 23.00 ♎

☾ △ ♄ 11.50

☾ 08.30

♀ Venus   ☉ Sun   △ Trine   ☌ Conjunction   ☷ Solar eclipse

♄ Saturn   ☐ Square   ✳ Sextile   ☍ Opposition   ☷ Lunar eclipse

February 2022

Monday 21

♎

☽ △ ☉ 14.30

☽ 08.50

Tuesday 22

Bring in bulbs for indoor flowering as they become ready.

♎

☽ 09.10

Wednesday 23

♎ 03.00 ♏

PM only

◐

☽ 09.40

☊ 07.00

Thursday 24

Start sowing salad crops and spinach and some early cabbage and Brussels sprouts.

♏

☽ 10.20

Friday 25

♏ 07.00 ♐

☽ 11.10

Change 07.00

Saturday 26

♐

AM only

☽ ✶ ☉ 05.10

☽ 12.20

℘ 22.00

Sunday 27

♐ 09.00 ♑

☽ ☌ ♀ 09.10

Change 09.00

☽ 13.30

● New Moon ◑ 1st quarter ☽ Moonrise ☊ North node 𝒜 Apogee
○ Full Moon ◐ 3rd quarter ☾ Moonset ☋ South node ℘ Perigee

February/March 2022

Monday 28

Parsnips, garlic, carrots and radishes might be sown today.

♑

☾ 14.50

Tuesday 1

St David's Day, the feast day of the patron saint of Wales. Mardi Gras, Shrove Tuesday

♑ 11.00 ♒

☾ 16.20

Change 11.00

Wednesday 2

Ash Wednesday, Lent begins: renounce something, such as eggs or cheese, to help the breeding farm animals.

♒

● 18.00

Thursday 3

The elements change in the afternoon from flower to leaf, so plan accordingly.

♒ 15.00 ♓

☽ 07.00

Change 15.00

Friday 4

Continue early sowings of salad crops and spinach, early cabbage and Brussels sprouts

♓

☽ 07.20

Saturday 5

Work with trees at noon, as the Moon chimes with Saturn.

♓ 21.00 ♈

☽ ⚹ ♄ 12.00

☽ 07.40

Sunday 6

Work with fruit trees in early morning.

♈

☽ 08.00

♈	♉	♊	♋	♌	♍
Aries	Taurus	Gemini	Cancer	Leo	Virgo
Fire	*Earth*	*Air*	*Water*	*Fire*	*Earth*

March 2022

Monday 7   ♈

☽ 08.20

☾ ⚹ ☉ 17.00

Tuesday 8   ♈ 07.00 ♉

Sow new Jerusalem artichokes today, keeping them a good 30 cm apart; also parsnips, garlic, carrots or radishes.

☊ 08.00

PM only

☽ 08.40

Wednesday 9   ♉

☽ 09.20

Thursday 10   ♉ 20.00 ♊

◑

☾ △ ♄ 10.50

☽ 09.50

𝒜 23.00

Change 20.00

Friday 11   ♊

Start some early cauliflowers around the Moonrise hour of 10–11 am.

☽ 10.40

Saturday 12   ♊

☽ 11.30

Sunday 13   ♊ 08.00 ♋

☽ 12.40

Change 08.00

♎ Libra Air	♏ Scorpio Water	♐ Sagittarius Fire	♑ Capricorn Earth	♒ Aquarius Air	♓ Pisces Water

March 2022

Monday 14

A good day for cabbages and leaf-crops, as Moon and Venus meet in the heavens.

♋

☽ 13.40

☽ ☌ ♀ 10.00

Tuesday 15

♋ 18.00 ♌

☽ 14.50

Change 18.00

Wednesday 16

♌

☽ 16.10

Thursday 17

St Patrick's Day

♌

☽ 17.20

Friday 18

Notice a surge in springtime growth around this Full Moon, especially if it has been raining on days before.

♌ 01.00 ♍

○ 07.00

Saturday 19

Dig over the garden and spread compost.

♍

☾ △ ♀ 08.50

☾ 06.30

Sunday 20

Spring Equinox. The planet Venus is at its highest in the morning sky.

♍ 06.00 ♎

☾ 06.50

Change 06.00

| ♀ Venus | ⊙ Sun | △ Trine | ♂ Conjunction | ◗ Solar eclipse |
| ♄ Saturn | ☐ Square | ✷ Sextile | ☍ Opposition | ◗ Lunar eclipse |

March 2022

Monday 21
It's Nowruz, the Persian New Year.

♎︎

☽ 07.20

☽ □ ♀ 16.30

Tuesday 22
Trim any tender crops damaged by frost or cold winds.

♎︎ 09.00 ♏︎

☽ 07.50

☡ 08.00

PM only

Wednesday 23

♏︎

☽ 08.20

𝑃 24.00

AM only

Thursday 24

♏︎ 12.00 ♐︎

☽ 09.10

☽ ✳ ♄ 07.10

AM

PM

Friday 25
Sow peas, beans or similar crops today.

♐︎

◐

☽ 10.10

Saturday 26

♐︎ 15.00 ♑︎

☽ 11.20

Change 15.00

Sunday 27
British Summer time begins.
Mothering Sunday – visit the church where you were baptised, or give Mum some flowers.

♑︎

☽ ✳ ☉ 13.30

☽ 13.40

● New Moon   ◐ 1st quarter   ☽ Moonrise   ☊ North node   𝐴 Apogee

○ Full Moon   ◑ 3rd quarter   ☽ Moonset   ☋ South node   𝑃 Perigee

March 2022

Monday 28

♑ 19.00 ♒   ☾ ☌ ♀ 14.50

☾ 15.00   ☾ ☌ ♄ 15.10

Change 19.00

Tuesday 29

It's time to prune late-flowering shrubs such as buddleia.

♒

☾ 16.20

Wednesday 30

Use the Moonset hour of 5–6 pm to plant out hardy perennials raised from seed.

♒

☾ 17.30

Thursday 31

♒ 00.00 ♓

☾ 18.50

Gardening Notes

♈	♉	♊	♋	♌	♍
Aries	Taurus	Gemini	Cancer	Leo	Virgo
Fire	Earth	Air	Water	Fire	Earth

April 2022

April Reminders

Friday 1
Hindu New Year

♓

● 07.00

Saturday 2
The Islamic month of Ramadan begins, when Muslims fast during hours of daylight.

♓ 07.00 ♈

☽ ⚹ ♀ 11.20

☽ 07.00

Change 07.00

Sunday 3
Plant late-flowering strawberries on suitable sites. Complete this month's fruit planting today.

♈

☽ 07.20

♎	♏	♐	♑	♒	♓
Libra	Scorpio	Sagittarius	Capricorn	Aquarius	Pisces
Air	*Water*	*Fire*	*Earth*	*Air*	*Water*

April 2022

Monday 4	♈ 17.00 ♉	☊ 14.00	No Planting
	☽ 07.50		✗

Tuesday 5

♉

☽ 08.10

plont ladish home.

Wednesday 6

Sow onion sets, maincrop carrots and globe beetroot as the Sun and Moon chime in the sky.

♉

☽ ⚹ ☉ 13.30

☽ 08.50

Thursday 7

♉ 05.00 ♊

plont cauli + carrots.

☽ 09.30

A 20.00

Change 05.00

Friday 8

The Sun is conjunct the asteroid Ceres today. Ceres was the Roman goddess of agriculture and fertility.

♊

☽ 10.20

Saturday 9

♊ 17.00 ♋

☽ 11.20

Change 17.00

Sunday 10

Palm Sunday, start of Holy Week.

♋

☽ 12.30

♀ Venus	☉ Sun	△ Trine	☌ Conjunction	● Solar eclipse
♄ Saturn	□ Square	⚹ Sextile	☍ Opposition	☾ Lunar eclipse

April 2022

Monday 11

♋

☽ 13.30

Tuesday 12

♋ 04.00 ♌

☽ 14.50

Wednesday 13

♌

☽ ☍ ♀ 06.30

☽ 16.00

Thursday 14
Maundy Thursday

♌ 11.00 ♍

☽ 17.10

Change 11.00

Friday 15
Good Friday. Some traditions say this is the best day to sow for extra-large crops, so sow root-crops today.

♍

☽ 18.30

Saturday 16
Feel the surging Full-Moon energies of springtime, when Nature is fertile and animals are mating.

♍ 16.00 ♎

☽ △ ♄ 14.10

○ 20.00

☽ 19.50

Change 16.00

Sunday 17
Easter Sunday. Plant out hardy perennials raised from seed. Dead-head daffodils as the flowers fade.

♎

☾ 06.20

● New Moon   ◑ 1st quarter   ☽ Moonrise   ♌ North node   𝒜 Apogee

○ Full Moon   ◐ 3rd quarter   ☾ Moonset   ☋ South node   𝒫 Perigee

April 2022

Monday 18
Easter Monday. Moon crosses its South Node today, so keep out of the garden.

♎ 18.00 ♏

☊ 15.00

☽ 06.50

No Planting

X

Tuesday 19
Keep out of the garden as the Moon comes nearest to Earth (perigee).

♏

☽ 07.20

𝒫 16.00

No Planting

X

Wednesday 20

♏ 19.00 ♐

☽ ✳ ♄ 18.20

☽ 08.00

Change 19.00

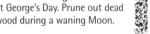

Thursday 21
Feel the harmony of the Sun–Moon trine. Plant late-flowering strawberries on suitable sites.

♐

☽ △ ☉ 06.40

☽ 09.00

Friday 22
View the Lyrids meteor shower tonight. Today is honoured as Earth Day: mull over the actions needed to save the Earth.

♐ 21.00 ♑

☽ ✳ ♀ 11.40

☽ 10.10

Saturday 23
St George's Day. Prune out dead wood during a waning Moon.

♑

◑

☽ 11.30

Sunday 24
Sow onion sets, maincrop carrots and globe beetroot at the Moonset hour around noon.

♑

☽ 12.50

| ♈ Aries *Fire* | ♉ Taurus *Earth* | ♊ Gemini *Air* | ♋ Cancer *Water* | ♌ Leo *Fire* | ♍ Virgo *Earth* |

April 2022

Monday 25
Set up roses around 2 pm. Plant out hardy perennials raised from seed.

♑ 01.00 ♒

☾ 14.10

Tuesday 26
Dead-head daffodils as the flowers fade.

♒

☾ 15.20

Wednesday 27

♒ 07.00 ♓

☾ ☌ ♀ 05.50

☾ 16.40

Change 07.00

Thursday 28
Prune trees on the waning Moon.

♓

☾ 17.50

Friday 29
Mercury should be well placed to view in the evening sky.

♓ 14.00 ♈

☾ ⚹ ♄ 14.20

☾ 19.00

AM

PM

Saturday 30
Partial solar eclipse. Stay out of the garden today.

♈

☉ ☽ 21.00

☾ 20.10

● 21.00

No Planting

✕

♎	♏	♐	♑	♒	♓
Libra	Scorpio	Sagittarius	Capricorn	Aquarius	Pisces
Air	*Water*	*Fire*	*Earth*	*Air*	*Water*

May 2022

May Reminders

Sunday 1

The Islamic month of Ramadan ends. On May Day, a May Queen honours the fertility of the Earth. Party all night, if you can.

♈

☽ 05.50

♌ 21.00

AM only

♀ Venus	☉ Sun	△ Trine	☌ Conjunction	Solar eclipse
♄ Saturn	□ Square	⚹ Sextile	☍ Opposition	Lunar eclipse

May 2022

Monday 2
Early May bank holiday. Prune lilac bushes after flowering.

♈ 00.00 ♉

☽ ⚹ ♀ 11.10

☽ 06.10

Tuesday 3
Draw up the soil around early potatoes.

♉

☽ 06.50

Wednesday 4

♉ 12.00 ♊

☽ △ ♄ 12.50

☽ 07.30

AM

PM

Thursday 5
The pagan spring fire-festival of Beltane marks the start of summer: young people dance and jump over the flames while elders drink mead.

♊ *plant basil, mint + parsley*

☽ □ ♀ 06.00

☽ 08.10 *outdoors.*

𝒜 14.00

Friday 6
Sow flowers in early morning, 8 am.

♊

☽ ⚹ ☉ 08.00

☽ 09.10 *Put the flowers out.*

Saturday 7
Graft during the waxing Moon.

♊ 01.00 ♋

☽ 10.10

Sunday 8
Plant out late summer cabbages and sow summer spinach.

♋

☽ 11.20

● New Moon   ◐ 1st quarter   ☽ Moonrise   ☊ North node   𝒜 Apogee
○ Full Moon   ◑ 3rd quarter   ☾ Moonset   ☋ South node   𝒫 Perigee

May 2022

Monday 9	♋ 13.00 ♌ ◑ ☽ 12.30	AM PM

Tuesday 10 Water fruit trees and bushes and feed apples and pears.	♌ *plant peas outside. @ home.* ☽ 13.40	

Wednesday 11 Continue to tend and water fruit trees and bushes.	♌ 21.00 ♍ ☽ △ ☉ 15.00 ☽ 14.50 *strawberries*	

Thursday 12	♍ ☽ 16.10	

Friday 13	♍ ☽ 17.20	

Saturday 14 Sow hardy and half-hardy annual flowers and plant out when all possible risk of frost has passed.	♍ 02.00 ♎ ☽ 18.50	

Sunday 15 Buddhist Wesak	♎ ☽ 20.10	

♈ Aries *Fire*	♉ Taurus *Earth*	♊ Gemini *Air*	♋ Cancer *Water*	♌ Leo *Fire*	♍ Virgo *Earth*

May 2022

Monday 16

Total lunar eclipse moments before sunrise. No garden work today. The Sun meets the binary star Algol.

♎ 03.00 ♏

○ ☌ 05.00

☊ 01.00

No Planting

Tuesday 17

♏

☽ 05.50

ℙ 16.00

☽ △ ♀ 16.30

No Planting

Wednesday 18

Sow runner beans and set up canes to support them.

♏ 04.00 ♐

☽ 06.50

☽ ✶ ♄ 05.00

Thursday 19

♐

☽ 08.00

Friday 20

Relax and feel the harmonious Sun–Moon trine. Sow maincrop beetroots, swedes and turnips and the last carrots on this root day.

♐ 04.00 ♑

☽ 09.10

☽ △ ☉ 13.00

Saturday 21

♑

☽ 10.30

Sunday 22

♑ 07.00 ♒

◑

☽ 11.50

☽ ☌ ♄ 08.20

Change 07.00

| ♎ Libra *Air* | ♏ Scorpio *Water* | ♐ Sagittarius *Fire* | ♑ Capricorn *Earth* | ♒ Aquarius *Air* | ♓ Pisces *Water* |

May 2022

Monday 23

♒

☾ 13.10

Tuesday 24

♒ 12.00 ♓

☾ 14.30

AM

PM

Wednesday 25

Sow spinach and cabbage this morning.

♓

☾✷☉ 06.00

☾ 15.40

Thursday 26

♓ 20.00 ♈

☾ 16.50

Change 20.00

Friday 27

♈

☾ 18.00

Saturday 28

Watch the thin sliver of the dying old Moon in the sunset.

♈

☾ 19.10

Sunday 29

The Moon is on its North Node; stay out of the garden.

♈ 07.00 ♉

☊ 04.00

☾ 20.20

PM only

May/June 2022

Monday 30
The Sun meets the rose-pink star Aldebaran, the 'Bulls-Eye', bringing good fortune.

♉

● 13.00

Tuesday 31
♉ 19.00 ♊

☽ 05.20

Change 19.00

Wednesday 1
Sow hardy wild flowers, and sow wallflowers around 4–5 pm. Hoe for weeds.

♊

☾ ⚹ ♀ 16.20

☽ 06.10

Thursday 2
Spring bank holiday

♊

☽ 07.00

𝒜 02.00

Friday 3
Platinum Jubilee bank holiday

♊ 08.00 ♋

☽ 08.00

Change 08.00

Saturday 4
Pick out shoots on aromatics such as rosemary to encourage growth.

♋

☽ 09.10

Sunday 5
♋ 20.00 ♌

☽ 10.10

Change 20.00

● New Moon   ◑ 1st quarter   ☽ Moonrise   ☊ North node   𝒜 Apogee
○ Full Moon   ◐ 3rd quarter   ☾ Moonset   ☋ South node   𝒫 Perigee

June 2022

Monday 6
Continue to sow dwarf and runner beans.

♌

☽ 11.20

Tuesday 7
Tend to fruit trees this morning.

♌

◑

☽ 12.30

☽ △ ♀ 05.10

Wednesday 8

♌ 06.00 ♍

☽ 13.50

Change 06.00

Thursday 9

♍

☽ 15.00

Friday 10
Work with fruit trees in the morning as the Moon chimes with Saturn.

♍ 12.00 ♎

☽ 16.20

☽ △ ♄ 13.30

AM

PM

Saturday 11

♎

☽ 17.40

Sunday 12

♎ 14.00 ♏

☊ 11.00

☽ 19.00

No Planting

♈ Aries *Fire*	♉ Taurus *Earth*	♊ Gemini *Air*	♋ Cancer *Water*	♌ Leo *Fire*	♍ Virgo *Earth*

June 2022

Monday 13

♏

☽ 20.20

Tuesday 14

It is a Supermoon tonight. The Full Moon occurs during its closest approach to Earth, its perigee.

♏ 14.00 ♐

☽ ✳ ♄ 15.40

○ 13.00

AM

PM

Wednesday 15

See how low the Full Moon is as it moves across the night sky. These could be the best days for the mating of animals.

♐

☽ 05.30

℘ 00.00

PM only

Thursday 16

♐ 13.00 ♑

☽ △ ♀ 10.10

☽ 06.50

AM

PM

Friday 17

Take softwood cuttings of shrubs to make new plants.

♑

☽ 08.10

Saturday 18

Excellent aspects for flower crops and trees in afternoon.

♑ 14.00 ♒

☽ □ ♀ 15.10

☽ 09.30

☽ ♂ ♄ 15.50

☽ △ ☉ 19.50

AM

PM

Sunday 19

♒

☽ 11.00

Libra
Air

♏
Scorpio
Water

♐
Sagittarius
Fire

♑
Capricorn
Earth

♒
Aquarius
Air

♓
Pisces
Water

June 2022

Monday 20

≈ 18.00 ♓

☾ 12.10

Change 18.00

Tuesday 21

Summer Solstice: celebrate the longest day with friends.

♓

◐

☾ 13.30

Wednesday 22

Pinch out shoots on aromatics such as rosemary to encourage growth.

♓

☾ 14.40

Thursday 23

Midsummer's Eve, St John's Eve

♓ 02.00 ♈

☾ ✶ ☉ 17.10

☾ 15.50

Friday 24

St John's Day. Look for the St John's Wort plant coming into blossom now; is it on time?

♈

☾ 17.00

Saturday 25

♈ 13.00 ♉

♋ 08.00

PM only

☾ 18.10

Sunday 26

♉

☾ ♂ ♄ 08.00

☾ 19.10

♀ Venus	☉ Sun	△ Trine	♂ Conjunction	◗ Solar eclipse
♄ Saturn	▢ Square	✶ Sextile	♂ Opposition	◖ Lunar eclipse

June 2022

Monday 27
☿

See last sliver of the dying old
Moon after sunset.

☾ 20.10

Tuesday 28
♉ 01.00 ♊

Sow hardy wild flowers, hoe for
weeds and sow wallflowers.

☾ 21.00

Wednesday 29
♓

● 04.00

☽ 05.00

𝒜 07.00

Thursday 30
♓ 14.00 ♋

☽ 05.50

AM

PM

Gardening Notes

● New Moon   ◐ 1st quarter   ☽ Moonrise   ♋ North node   𝒜 Apogee

○ Full Moon   ◑ 3rd quarter   ☾ Moonset   ☋ South node   𝒫 Perigee

July 2022

July Reminders

Friday 1	♋	
	☽ 07.00	
Saturday 2	♋	
	☽ 08.00	
Sunday 3	♋ 02.00 ♌	
	☽ 09.10	

♈	♉	♊	♋	♌	♍
Aries	Taurus	Gemini	Cancer	Leo	Virgo
Fire	*Earth*	*Air*	*Water*	*Fire*	*Earth*

July 2022

Monday 4
Aphelion at 8 am, when the Earth is at its furthest point from the Sun.

♌

☽ 10.20

☽ ⚹ ☉ 14.00

Tuesday 5
♌ 12.00 ♍

☽ 11.30

AM

PM

Wednesday 6
♍

☽ 12.40

Thursday 7
♍ 20.00 ♎

◐

☽ 14.00

☽ △ ♀ 06.50

Change 20.00

Friday 8
Use the Moonrise hour of 5 pm to plant flowers.

♎

☽ 15.10

Saturday 9
Sow flowering plants around noon, enjoy the harmony of a Sun–Moon trine.

♎ 24.00 ♏

☽ 16.30

☽ △ ☉ 12.10

AM only

☊ 18.00

Sunday 10
♏

☽ 18.00

♎	♏	♐	♑	♒	♓
Libra	Scorpio	Sagittarius	Capricorn	Aquarius	Pisces
Air	Water	Fire	Earth	Air	Water

July 2022

Monday 11
♏︎

☽ 19.10

Tuesday 12
It's holiday time, enjoy a dinner outdoors and appreciate how the silvery Full Moon rises in the East as the golden Sun sets in the West.

♏︎ 01.00 ♐︎

☽ 20.20

Wednesday 13
It is a Supermoon tonight. The Full Moon occurs during its closest approach to Earth, its perigee.

♐︎

○ 20.00

♇ 10.00

No Planting

X

Thursday 14
Be warned that floods may take place during the Full Moon at perigee.

♐︎ 00.00 ♑︎

☾ 05.40

Friday 15
♑︎ 24.00 ♒︎

☾ 07.00

Saturday 16
A fine flower day as the Moon chimes with Venus this morning.

♒︎

☾ △ ♀ 05.40

☾ 08.30

Sunday 17
Prune apple and pear trees today, and thin early dessert apples.

♒︎

☾ 09.50

| ♀ Venus | ☉ Sun | △ Trine | ♂ Conjunction | Solar eclipse |
| ♄ Saturn | □ Square | ✳ Sextile | ☍ Opposition | Lunar eclipse |

July 2022

Monday 18

≈ 02.00 ♓

☾ 11.10

Tuesday 19

Sow leaf crops around noon, especially lettuce and greens for the winter.

♓

☾ 12.30

Wednesday 20

♓ 08.00 ♈

☾ ✳ ♄ 07.30

◑

☾ 13.40

Change 08.00

Thursday 21

♈

☾ 14.50

Friday 22

♈ 19.00 ♉

☊ 10.00

☾ 16.00

No Planting

X

Saturday 23

Sow winter radish and dig up early potatoes if they are ready.

♉

☾ ✳ ☉ 07.00

☾ 17.10

Sunday 24

♉

☾ 18.10

● New Moon   ◑ 1st quarter   ☽ Moonrise   ☊ North node   ⒜ Apogee

○ Full Moon   ◐ 3rd quarter   ☾ Moonset   ☋ South node   ℗ Perigee

July 2022

Monday 25
See the last sliver of the old Moon at sunset.

♉ 07.00 ♊

☾ △ ♄ 05.30

☾ 19.00

Change 07.00

Tuesday 26
Lift and divide hellebores in a moist, shady spot.

♊

☾ ♂ ♀ 15.50

☾ 19.40

⚶ 11.00

Wednesday 27

♊ 20.00 ♋

☾ 20.20

Change 20.00

Thursday 28
Crops harvested at New Moon will keep best.

♋

● 19.00

Friday 29
Sow lettuce and greens for the winter, leeks, late Brussels sprouts, winter cabbage and sprouting and spring broccoli.

♋

☽ 05.50

Saturday 30
Islamic New Year

♋ 08.00 ♌

☽ 07.00

Change 08.00

Sunday 31
Use the Moonrise hour of 8 am for fruit, taking cuttings and propagating during the waxing Moon.

♌

☽ 08.10

♈	♉	♊	♋	♌	♍
Aries	Taurus	Gemini	Cancer	Leo	Virgo
Fire	*Earth*	*Air*	*Water*	*Fire*	*Earth*

August 2022

Monday 1
Summer bank holiday in Scotland

♌ 18.00 ♍

☽ 09.20

Change 18.00

Tuesday 2

♍

☽ 10.30

Wednesday 3
Sow root crops around noon.

♍

☽ 11.50

Thursday 4
Transplant flower seedlings during the waxing Moon. Plant daffodils and take cuttings from rambling roses.

♍ 02.00 ♎

☽ 13.00

Friday 5
Sow wallflowers and sweet Williams for next year and set out seedlings of biennials.

♎

☊ 22.00

AM only

◐

☽ 14.20

Saturday 6

♎ 08.00 ♏

☽ △ ♀ 06.00

Change 08.00

☽ 15.30

Sunday 7
Today is Lammas, the old English festival to mark the wheat harvest. Mark the occasion with a barbecue.

♏

☽ △ ☉ 19.20

☽ 16.50

♎	♏	♐	♑	♒	♓
Libra	Scorpio	Sagittarius	Capricorn	Aquarius	Pisces
Air	*Water*	*Fire*	*Earth*	*Air*	*Water*

August 2022

Monday 8

♏ 10.00 ♐

☽ ⚹ ♄ 07.10

☽ 18.00

Change 10.00

Tuesday 9

Prepare the ground for new fruit stocks, and complete the planting of strawberry runners.

♐

☽ 19.00

Wednesday 10

♐ 10.00 ♑

☽ ☍ ♀ 17.40

AM only

☽ 19.40

℗ 18.00

Thursday 11

Animals are fertile now, this Full Moon is the best time for mating them.

♑

☽ 20.20

Friday 12

The Perseids meteor shower, coming from the Perseus constellation, might not be visible tonight due to the Full Moon.

♑ 10.00 ♒

☾ ☌ ♄ 07.00

○ 03.00

Change 10.00

☾ 06.00

Saturday 13

The planet Saturn would be at its brightest tonight, but its view is obstructed by the fully illuminated Moon.

♒

☾ 07.20

Sunday 14

♒ 12.00 ♓

AM

☾ 08.50

PM

♀ Venus	☉ Sun	△ Trine	♂ Conjunction	◗ Solar eclipse
♄ Saturn	☐ Square	⚹ Sextile	☍ Opposition	◗ Lunar eclipse

August 2022

Monday 15
Sow winter spinach, spring cabbage and hardy lettuce today.

♓

☾ 10.10

Tuesday 16

♓ 17.00 ♈

☾ 11.20

☾ ⚹ ♄ 12.10

☾ △ ☉ 15.50

Change 17.00

Wednesday 17
Prune the fruited shoots of peach and plum trees.

♈

☾ 12.40

Thursday 18
Keep out of the garden today, a node crossing at noon is too disturbing for plant life.

♈

☊ 12.00

☾ 13.50

No Planting

X

Friday 19
Water your garden in the afternoon.

♈ 02.00 ♉

◑

☾ 15.00

Saturday 20

♉

☾ 16.00

☾ ⚹ ♀ 10.10

Sunday 21

♉ 14.00 ♊

☾ 16.50

☾ △ ♄ 08.00

AM

PM

● New Moon   ◑ 1st quarter   ☽ Moonrise   ☊ North node   ⚲ Apogee
○ Full Moon   ◐ 3rd quarter   ☾ Moonset   ☋ South node   ℗ Perigee

August 2022

Monday 22

The Sun meets Regulus, for millennia the brightest star in the constellation Leo; it moved on into Virgo recently, the sign of ecology.

Ⅱ

☾ 17.40

♃ 23.00

Tuesday 23

Prune rambling roses.

Ⅱ

☾ 18.20

Wednesday 24

Ⅱ 02.00 ♋

☾ 18.50

Thursday 25

Sow winter spinach, spring cabbage and hardy lettuce today.

♋

☾ 19.20

Friday 26

Crops harvested at the New Moon will keep best. Dry out herbs before storing them.

♋ 14.00 ♌

☾ 19.40

AM

PM

Saturday 27

Re-pot tomatoes sown in June, prepare the ground for planting new fruit stocks, and complete the planting of strawberry runners.

♌

● 09.00

Sunday 28

♌ 24.00 ♍

☽ 07.10

♈	♉	Ⅱ	♋	♌	♍
Aries	Taurus	Gemini	Cancer	Leo	Virgo
Fire	*Earth*	*Air*	*Water*	*Fire*	*Earth*

August 2022

Monday 29
Summer bank holiday

♍

☽ 08.20

Tuesday 30

♍

☽ 09.40

Wednesday 31

♍ 08.00 ♎

☽ ⚹ ♀ 07.10

☽ 10.50

Change 08.00

Gardening Notes

♎	♏	♐	♑	♒	♓
Libra	Scorpio	Sagittarius	Capricorn	Aquarius	Pisces
Air	*Water*	*Fire*	*Earth*	*Air*	*Water*

September 2022

September Reminders

Thursday 1
Take rose cuttings in the morning.

♎︎

☽ 12.10

☽ ⚹ ☉ 10.20

♉︎ 22.00

AM only

Friday 2

♎︎ 13.00 ♏︎

☽ 13.20

☽ □ ♀ 18.20

AM

PM

Saturday 3

♏︎

◐

☽ 14.40

Sunday 4

♏︎ 17.00 ♐︎

☽ 15.50

☽ ⚹ ♄ 10.50

Change 17.00

| ♀ Venus | ☉ Sun | △ Trine | ☌ Conjunction | ● Solar eclipse |
| ♄ Saturn | □ Square | ⚹ Sextile | ☍ Opposition | ☽ Lunar eclipse |

September 2022

Monday 5
Sow herbs or seed crops over the Moonrise hour of 5 pm.

♐

☽ 16.50

Tuesday 6
Prepare the ground for planting new fruit stocks.

♐ 19.00 ♑

☽ 17.40

Change 19.00

Wednesday 7

♑

AM only

☽ 18.10

ℙ 19.00

Thursday 8

♑ 20.00 ♒

☽☌♄ 13.30

☽ 18.40

Change 20.00

Friday 9
Transplant flower seedlings at around 2–3 pm.

♒

☽☍♀ 14.40

☽ 19.10

Saturday 10
At dusk, see the golden orb of the Harvest Moon hanging low above the horizon. Harvest around now for ripe crops that will go straight to market.

♒ 22.00 ♓

○ 11.00

Sunday 11
Sow annuals in the greenhouse for a spring display.

♓

☾ 07.40

● New Moon   ◐ 1st quarter   ☽ Moonrise   ☊ North node   𝒜 Apogee

○ Full Moon   ◑ 3rd quarter   ☾ Moonset   ☋ South node   ℙ Perigee

September 2022

Monday 12

Sow parsley and chervil and varieties of lettuce for overwintering under cloches.

♓

☽ 09.00

☾ ⚹ ♄ 18.30

Tuesday 13

Farmers, harvest the golden grain during a waning Moon.

♓ 02.00 ♈

☽ 10.10

Wednesday 14

♈

☽ 11.30

☾ △ ♀ 09.40

☊ 16.00

No Planting

X

Thursday 15

Venus fades from view as the Morning Star.

♈ 10.00 ♉

☽ 12.40

☾ △ ☉ 06.30

Change 10.00

Friday 16

♉

☽ 13.50

Saturday 17

♉ 21.00 ♊

◑

☽ 14.50

☾ △ ♄ 12.00

Sunday 18

Tend to perennial flower crops in the afternoon.

♊

☽ 15.40

♈	♉	♊	♋	♌	♍
Aries	Taurus	Gemini	Cancer	Leo	Virgo
Fire	*Earth*	*Air*	*Water*	*Fire*	*Earth*

September 2022

Monday 19

Transplant flower seedlings, plant daffodils and take cuttings from rambler roses.

Ⅱ

☾ 16.20

♌ 16.00

Tuesday 20

Ⅱ 10.00 ♋

☾ ⚹ ☉ 17.00

☾ 16.50

Change 10.00

Wednesday 21

Sow parsley and chervil under cloches.

♋

☾ 17.20

Thursday 22

Autumn Equinox when days and nights have equal length: the traditional story of Demeter and Persephone belongs here.

♋ 22.00 ♌

☾ 17.50

Friday 23

Pick early apples and pears for storage while slightly under-ripe. Re-pot tomatoes sown in June.

♌

☾ 18.10

Saturday 24

Farmers, harvesting of fruit to store over winter is best now, at the New Moon.

♌

☾ 18.30

Sunday 25

Jupiter is at its brightest in the night sky on this new Moon. Jewish New Year.

♌ 07.00 ♍

☾ ☌ ♀ 08.20

● 23.00

Change 07.00

☾ 18.40

♎	♏	♐	♑	♒	♓
Libra	Scorpio	Sagittarius	Capricorn	Aquarius	Pisces
Air	Water	Fire	Earth	Air	Water

September 2022

Monday 26	♍︎ ☽ 07.20	
Tuesday 27	♍︎ 14.00 ♎︎ ☽ 08.40	AM PM
Wednesday 28	♎︎ ☽ 09.50	
Thursday 29 Michaelmas Day	♎︎ 19.00 ♏︎ ☋ 01.00 ☽ 11.10	PM only
Friday 30	♏︎ ☽⚹♀ 07.00 ☽ 12.30 ☽⚹☉ 18.10	

Gardening Notes

♀ Venus   ☉ Sun   △ Trine   ☌ Conjunction   ◗ Solar eclipse
♄ Saturn   ☐ Square   ⚹ Sextile   ☍ Opposition   ◓ Lunar eclipse

October 2022

October Reminders

Saturday 1

♏ 23.00 ♐

☽ ✶ ♄ 13.50

☽ 13.40

Sunday 2

Harvest Festival is celebrated
this Sunday. Graft fruit trees this
afternoon.

♐

☽ 14.40

● New Moon ◑ 1st quarter ☽ Moonrise ☊ North node 𝒜 Apogee
○ Full Moon ◑ 3rd quarter ☾ Moonset ☋ South node 𝒫 Perigee

October 2022

Monday 3

Pick late tomatoes and let them ripen in trays. Work on any fruit trees, especially between 3–4 pm.

♐

◑

☽ 15.30

Tuesday 4

♐ 02.00 ♑

☽ 16.10

P 18.00

AM only

Wednesday 5

A good day to prepare land and for digging compost into the soil.

♑

☽ 16.50

☽ △ ☉ 07.30

☽ ☌ ♄ 19.00

Thursday 6

Plant out bulbs on rock gardens or between herbaceous plants this afternoon.

♑ 04.00 ♒

☽ 17.10

Friday 7

♒

☽ 17.30

Saturday 8

♒ 07.00 ♊

☽ 17.50

Change 07.00

Sunday 9

Start planting winter lettuce around 3 pm, and force-grow rhubarb in a warm greenhouse.

♊

○ 22.00

☽ 18.10

☽ ☍ ♀ 15.20

♈	♉	♊	♋	♌	♍
Aries	Taurus	Gemini	Cancer	Leo	Virgo
Fire	Earth	Air	Water	Fire	Earth

October 2022

Monday 10

♓ 12.00 ♈

☾ 07.50

AM

PM

Tuesday 11

Cut out fruited blackberry and loganberry canes.

♈

☊ 23.00

☾ 09.10

AM only

Wednesday 12

♈ 19.00 ♉

☾ 10.20

Change 19.00

Thursday 13

Dig up maincrop potatoes and lift and store beetroot.

♉

☾ 11.30

Friday 14

♉

☾ 12.30

☾ △ ♄ 18.30

☾ △ ♀ 19.50

Saturday 15

♉ 06.00 ♊

☾ 13.30

Change 06.00

Sunday 16

Prune rambling roses, prepare new rose beds for planting. Plant lily of the valley. Plant out herbaceous perennials..

♊

☾ 14.20

♎	♏	♐	♑	♒	♓
Libra	Scorpio	Sagittarius	Capricorn	Aquarius	Pisces
Air	*Water*	*Fire*	*Earth*	*Air*	*Water*

October 2022

Monday 17
The Sun passes by Spica today, the benevolent star of the grain harvest.

♊ 18.00 ♋

◐

☾ 14.50

♐ 11.00

☾ □ ♀ 15.10

Change 18.00

Tuesday 18

♋

☾ 15.20

Wednesday 19

♋

☾ 15.50

Thursday 20
Venus meets the Sun in our sky today.

♋ 06.00 ♌

☾ 16.10

☾ ⚹ ♀ 10.10

☾ ⚹ ☉ 11.40

Change 06.00

Friday 21
Pick late tomatoes and let them ripen in trays. Work on any fruit trees, especially between 4–5 pm.

♌

☾ 16.30

Saturday 22

♌ 16.00 ♍

☾ 16.50

Change 16.00

Sunday 23
At the dark of the Moon, pick crops to store over winter.

♍

☾ 17.10

♀ Venus   ☉ Sun   △ Trine   ☌ Conjunction   ● Solar eclipse

♄ Saturn   □ Square   ⚹ Sextile   ☍ Opposition   ● Lunar eclipse

October 2022

Monday 24
The Indian festival of Diwali begins; light some candles to celebrate.

♍ 22.00 ♎

☾ 17.30

☾ △ ♄ 12.10

Tuesday 25
This partial solar eclipse phenomena is visible from the UK and Europe. Protect your eyes when watching it. No garden work today.

♎

● ◐ 12.00

☾ ☌ ♀ 13.00

No Planting

✗

Wednesday 26
Tend to flowers in the greenhouse.

♎

☽ 08.50

☋ 08.00

PM only

Thursday 27
Plant herbaceous perennials and deciduous trees, but avoid frosty conditions.

♎ 02.00 ♏

☽ 10.10

Friday 28
Diwali ends. Tend to trees this afternoon as the Moon chimes with Saturn.

♏

☽ 11.30

☽ ⚹ ♄ 19.20

Saturday 29

♏ 05.00 ♐

☽ 12.40

𝑃 16.00

No Planting

✗

Sunday 30
End of British Summer Time: clocks go back one hour.

♐

☽ 12.30

● New Moon ◐ 1st quarter ☽ Moonrise ☊ North node 𝐴 Apogee
○ Full Moon ◐ 3rd quarter ☾ Moonset ☋ South node 𝑃 Perigee

October 2022

Monday 31

Halloween, traditionally a time of otherworldly interference in human affairs.

♐ 06.00 ♑

☽ 13.20

Change 06.00

Gardening Notes

November 2022

Tuesday 1
All Saints' Day

♑

◑

☽ 13.50

Wednesday 2

♑ 09.00 ♒

☽ 14.20

Change 09.00

Thursday 3
Cut back and tidy any flowering plants in the afternoon. In the greenhouse, start forcing bulbs and sow seed of most alpines.

♒

☽ △ ☉ 14.00

☽ 14.40

☽ △ ♀ 19.40

Friday 4
Clear fallen leaves away from small plants so they are not too damp.

♒ 13.00 ♓

☽ 15.00

AM

PM

Saturday 5
Bonfire Night. Take cuttings of bay and rue. Place in pots of sand; divide roots of mint, re-potting some for the greenhouse.

♓

☽ 15.20

Sunday 6

♓ 19.00 ♈

☽ ⚹ ♄ 08.40

☽ 15.40

Change 19.00

♎	♏	♐	♑	♒	♓
Libra	Scorpio	Sagittarius	Capricorn	Aquarius	Pisces
Air	Water	Fire	Earth	Air	Water

November 2022

Monday 7

The pagan quarter-day of Samhain: a gathering of the clans before winter begins.

♈

☽ 16.00

Tuesday 8

Total lunar eclipse. Stay out of the garden.

♈

○ ☄ 11.00

☊ 06.00

☾ ☍ ♀ 19.50

No Planting

✗

Wednesday 9

Dig new beds and borders for winter weathering.

♈ 02.00 ♉

☾ 08.10

Thursday 10

Make a compost bin for what is raked up in the garden.

♉

☾ 09.20

Friday 11

♉ 13.00 ♊

☾ 10.20

AM

PM

Saturday 12

Prick out any perennials you have raised in the greenhouse and sow winter bedding plants.

♊

☾ 11.10

Sunday 13

Remembrance Sunday. Use today for indoor flower work. Also plant tulips, hardy climbers and roses.

♊

☾ △ ☉ 19.20

☾ 11.50

♀ Venus   ⊙ Sun   △ Trine   ♂ Conjunction   ☄ Solar eclipse

♄ Saturn   □ Square   ✳ Sextile   ☍ Opposition   ☄ Lunar eclipse

November 2022

Monday 14
Use the Moonrise hour to lift chicory and asparagus.

♊ 01.00 ♋

☾ △ ♀ 07.50

☾ 12.20

𝒜 07.00

Tuesday 15
Prune trees.

♋

☾ 12.50

Wednesday 16

♋ 13.00 ♌

◑

☾ 13.10

AM

PM

Thursday 17
Sow fruit crops in the greenhouse for next year, around 1–2 pm.

♌

☾ 13.30

Friday 18
Plant fruit trees and bushes, soaking dry tree-roots before planting, and prune fruit trees after planting. Stake trees.

♌ 24.00 ♍

☾ 13.50

Saturday 19

♍

☾ ✶ ☉ 05.00

☾ 14.10

☾ ✶ ♀ 19.20

Sunday 20

♍

☾ 14.30

● New Moon   ◐ 1st quarter   ☽ Moonrise   ♋ North node   𝒜 Apogee
○ Full Moon   ◑ 3rd quarter   ☾ Moonset   ☋ South node   𝒫 Perigee

November 2022

Monday 21

♍ 07.00 ♎

☾ 14.50

Change 07.00

Tuesday 22

♎

♉ 16.00

☾ 15.10

No Planting

✗

Wednesday 23

♎ 11.00 ♏

● 23.00

☾ 15.40

Change 11.00

Thursday 24

Lift chicory and asparagus, harvest crops for winter storage.

♏

☽ ♂ ♀ 13.30

☽ 08.10

Friday 25

♏ 12.00 ♐

☽ 09.20

AM

PM

Saturday 26

Prune any late vines in the morning.

♐

☽ 10.20

♇ 02.00

PM only

Sunday 27

♐ 13.00 ♑

☽ 11.10

AM

PM

♈	♉	♊	♋	♌	♍
Aries	Taurus	Gemini	Cancer	Leo	Virgo
Fire	*Earth*	*Air*	*Water*	*Fire*	*Earth*

November 2022

Monday 28

♑

☽ ✶ ☉ 08.10

☽ 11.50

Tuesday 29

♑ 14.00 ♒

☽ ☌ ♄ 06.50

☽ 12.20

AM

PM

Wednesday 30

St Andrew's Day is celebrated in Scotland. Finish planting roses and prune back established rose beds.

♒

◑

☽ 12.40

Gardening Notes

♎	♏	♐	♑	♒	♓
Libra	Scorpio	Sagittarius	Capricorn	Aquarius	Pisces
Air	*Water*	*Fire*	*Earth*	*Air*	*Water*

December 2022

December Reminders

Thursday 1

♒ 18.00 ♓

☽ □ ♀ 09.10

☽ 13.00

Change 18.00

Friday 2

Venus re-appears as the Evening Star on around this date.

♓

☽ 13.20

Saturday 3

♓

☽ ⚹ ♄ 17.10

☽ 13.40

Sunday 4

Advent Sunday; Christmas decorations can go up now.

♓ 01.00 ♈

☽ 14.00

| ♀ Venus | ☉ Sun | △ Trine | ♂ Conjunction | ◖ Solar eclipse |
| ♄ Saturn | □ Square | ⚹ Sextile | ☍ Opposition | ◗ Lunar eclipse |

December 2022

Monday 5

♈

☊ 13.00

☽ 14.30

No Planting

X

Tuesday 6

St Nicholas's Day

♈ 10.00 ♉

☽ 14.50

Change 10.00

Wednesday 7

See how high the midwinter Full Moon rises in the midnight sky!

♉

☽ 15.30

Thursday 8

The planet Mars would be at its brightest tonight, but the Full Moon steals the show.

♉ 20.00 ♊

☾ △ ♄ 12.40

○ 04.00

☾ 08.10

Change 20.00

Friday 9

Pot on Autumn-sown sweet peas. Plant shrubs if the weather permits.

♊

☾ ☌ ♀ 05.30

☾ 09.00

Saturday 10

♊

☾ 09.50

Sunday 11

♊ 08.00 ♋

☾ 10.20

Change 08.00

● New Moon ◑ 1st quarter ☽ Moonrise ♌ North node 𝒜 Apogee
○ Full Moon ◐ 3rd quarter ☾ Moonset ☋ South node 𝒫 Perigee

December 2022

Monday 12

Trim back lawn edges to make the garden tidy.

♋

☾ 10.50

♐ 00.00

Tuesday 13

Plant new hedges, shrubs and trees.

♋ 21.00 ♌

☾ △ ☉ 15.50

☾ 11.20

Wednesday 14

The Geminids meteor shower may reach its maximum during this dark night, weather permitting.

♌

☾ 11.40

Thursday 15

Cut down any old raspberry canes.

♌

☾ 12.00

Friday 16

♌ 09.00 ♍

◑

☾ 12.10

Change 09.00

Saturday 17

Sow carrots in frames. Check over any stored corms or tubers for signs of mould.

♍

☾ 12.30

Sunday 18

♍ 17.00 ♎

☾ △ ♄ 11.30

☾ 12.50

Change 17.00

♈	♉	♊	♋	♌	♍
Aries	Taurus	Gemini	Cancer	Leo	Virgo
Fire	*Earth*	*Air*	*Water*	*Fire*	*Earth*

December 2022

Monday 19

♎

☾ 13.10

Tuesday 20

♎ 21.00 ♏

☊ 02.00

☾ 13.40

PM only

Wednesday 21

Winter Solstice, the shortest day and longest night. The Sun now crosses over the 'Galactic Equator' in the Milky Way.

♏

☾ 14.10

Thursday 22

♏ 23.00 ♐

☾ ⚹ ♄ 18.20

☾ 15.00

Friday 23

Sow melons for early crop, and early peas and beans for cropping under glass. Sow tomatoes for a summer crop in the greenhouse.

♐

● 10.00

Saturday 24

Christmas Eve

♐ 22.00 ♑

☽ ☌ ♀ 12.20

☽ 09.00

℘ 08.00

PM only

Sunday 25

Christmas Day and the twelve Holy Nights begin.

♑

☽ 09.50

♎	♏	♐	♑	♒	♓
Libra	Scorpio	Sagittarius	Capricorn	Aquarius	Pisces
Air	Water	Fire	Earth	Air	Water

December 2022

Monday 26

Boxing Day. Examine stored vegetables and remove any that are diseased. Dig over the ground.

♑ 22.00 ♒

☽ ☌ ♄ 18.20

☽ 10.20

Tuesday 27

Substitute bank holiday for Christmas Day. Enjoy the harmonious Sun–Moon aspect this afternoon.

♒

☽ ✶ ☉ 17.20

☽ 10.50

Wednesday 28

♒

☽ 11.10

Thursday 29

♒ 00.00 ♓

☽ 11.30

Friday 30

♓

◑

☽ 11.50

Saturday 31

Prune new fruited shoots of peach and plum trees.

♓ 06.00 ♈

☽ 12.10

Change 06.00

♀ Venus   ☉ Sun   △ Trine   ☌ Conjunction   ◔ Solar eclipse

♄ Saturn   □ Square   ✶ Sextile   ☍ Opposition   ☾ Lunar eclipse

The Seasons of
2022

Young Spring was there, his head encircled with a flowery garland, and Summer, lightly clad, crowned with a wreath of corn ears; Autumn too, stained purple with treading out the vintage, and icy Winter, with white and shaggy locks.

Ovid

s the year dawns you can just see Venus as the Evening Star, although it will soon fade from view around 3 January. Invisibly it meets the Sun on 8 January and is then at its closest to the Earth. The other opener of the year, *Perihelion*, falls on 4 January, when the Earth is at its closest to the Sun in the deep midwinter – at least, in the Northern hemisphere – ironically given how cold it is at this time. Venus re-emerges as the Morning Star around 14 January. The lovely old English word for this was used by Tolkein in his ring epic for the morning star: 'Hail *Eärendil*, brightest of stars'. Farmers up before dawn may wish to meditate upon the old Roman name of *Lucifer*, which meant 'light-bringer': at Venus's pre-dawn appearance the stars were put to flight. Eventually it will fade from view later in the year, around 15 September. It will reappear as the Evening Star again around 2 December. Perhaps consider holding a winter party in early December so that your guests can admire the Evening Star?

For pagans, February opens with the Imbolc fire-festival on 3 February. This signifies the promise or the first glimpse of spring, when the first snowdrops appear, when ewes start to lactate and will soon give birth to the spring lambs. It was the feast of the Celtic goddess Brid and farmers would then 'beat the bounds' of their land. Around this time there is Groundhog Day in the US and Candlemas in the Christian calendar, which both signify winter's end. Many such festivals were absorbed into the Christian traditions, so there was a melding of pagan and Christian significance. Rustic proverbs cluster around this day, for example from Germany: 'The badger peeps out of his hole on Candlemas day/And if he finds snow, walks abroad/ But if he sees the sun shining/Draws back into his hole'.

The Chinese New Year, which is always on the New Moon closest to Imbolc, comes early on 1 February. 2022 is the Year of the Tiger. Pay off your debts, clear out the clutter from your home and, if you can, join in the festival of the Red Dragon in your nearest Chinatown! A month later Mardi Gras is celebrated – Shrove Tuesday in the Christian calendar – and that comes after the next New Moon. A New Moon is a proper time for beginnings.

The Persian New Year is sensibly fixed on to the spring equinox 20 March. A few days earlier there comes the festival of St Patrick's Day then Mothering Sunday just afterwards, but our calendar is more focused on lunar-defined events that make up the ancient sacred calendars of humanity. Christian Holy Week centres around the Full Moon of 16 April, after the spring equinox. Two weeks before that the Hindu New Year, 1 April, falls on the same New Moon as Ramadan, a time of fast for Muslims who are not allowed to eat or drink while the Sun is above the horizon. That holy month starts when the first sliver of the New Moon is seen, which is here one day after the astronomical New Moon.

May and July have 'Supermoons', when the Moon appears extra large, due to the Full Moon being on or near to its perigee.

The pagan fire-festival of Beltane falls on 5 May. Have a bonfire if you can, but you may prefer to celebrate it a few days earlier on the bank holiday. This 'quarter-day' midway between the solstices and equinoxes is a time to mull over the eightfold structure of the year: this festival is the start of summer, not the middle of spring! It is a life-affirming fire-festival, to honour the fertility of spring. Farm animals lactate and sheep and cattle are put out to summer pastures. Be up to greet the dawn and early-morning mists – after an all-night party, if you can! See if your community can manage a May Queen and a maypole, to invoke a festive spirit.

The longest day on midsummer solstice chimes on 21 June, when Earth and Sun align with the galaxy, on that longest day and the Sun crosses over the Galactic Equator. If you have a St John's Wort plant, check if it has opened up as it should on St John's Day, 24 June. St John's Wort is a traditional remedy for depression. Note how this day is three days after the summer solstice, just as Christmas comes three days after the winter solstice. This is when the Sun starts to move again as seen on the horizon – it 'stands still' on the solstice, that's what the word means.

July begins with Aphelion, when the Earth is furthest away from the Sun in its yearly course. Here is another paradox: we feel the warmest summer heat when the planet is furthest from the Sun. Try to enjoy a summer barbecue around Lammas-time in early August which is a few days before the Full Moon this year. Lammas is a summer holiday period, a 'gathering of the tribes' and the word alludes to the loaf made from the first new wheat, so this summer's-end festival marks the start of the harvest and the end of the crop-circle season! On 13 August watch the Perseids meteor shower in the early hours after midnight.

In mid-September comes the Harvest Moon, big and yellow near to the horizon. Two weeks later comes the Jewish New Year at the New Moon on the autumn equinox. This tips us into the dark half of the year: the equinox period is a time to recall the ancient Greek mystery-story of how Demeter, the earth or corn-goddess, loses her lovely daughter Persephone, who will not reappear until spring.

The start of October brings the Hunter's Moon rising, in the 'season of mists and mellow fruitfulness'. Around then on the first Sunday of October is the Harvest Festival when we give thanks for the fruits of the Earth. The Sun is passing through the sidereal sign of the Balance over this period, until 17 October – that's the same zodiac system used in this calendar for the Moon.

For Samhain, (pronounced 'sawain') the start of the Celtic New Year on 7 November, our modern equivalents are Hallowe'en and Bonfire Night. This was the traditional time for the last gathering of clans before winter. Nature dies back for another year, bringing an other-worldly flavour to this time of supernatural interference in human affairs: ghosts, ghouls and divination. A week later, try to see little Mercury in the sky after sunset.

Over the Christmas period all the life-forces of Nature have withdrawn into the ground and we can experience the wonderful purity of a snow-clad landscape, and meditate upon the crystalline perfection of a snowflake.

Sacred Moons of 2022

In our multi-cultural society, it makes sense to honour the sacred moons of different cultures. The calendars of several of the great religions are founded on the lunar cycle and lunar-based sacred calendars still exist around the world. Many cultures begin their year on a New Moon, which is the proper time for new beginnings. The calendar gives these dates for five different world religions: Islam, Judaism, Christianity, Buddhism and Hinduism, as well as the Chinese State calendar. Let's make the honouring of these sacred moons of different cultures a socially cohesive force in the modern world.

Through these sacred events one can experience the concept of the dark time of New Moon as a beginning. In today's electric-light society one is hardly able to sense the significance of this time of the month when the Moon cannot be seen by day or night. Mental health, balance in life and happiness are all assisted by living more in tune with the lunar calendar

Here are the 'sacred moons' of 2022, i.e. the Full Moons of Easter and Wesak (Buddhist) plus other New Moon festivals.

Chinese New Year	1 February, Year of the Tiger	New Moon on 1 February
Hindu New Year	1 April	New Moon on 1 April
Easter Sunday	17 April	Full Moon on 16 April
Buddhist Wesak	15 May	Full Moon on 16 May
Start of Ramadan	2 April	New Moon on 1 April
Jewish New Year	25 September	New Moon on 25 September
Muslim New Year	29 July	New Moon on 28 July
Hindu Diwali	24 October	New Moon on 25 November